Memory Miracle
Strategies For Success In Life And Learning

Pooja Agarwal

Ik Ink of Knowledge
.com

Title: Memory Miracle: Strategies For Success In Life And Learning

Author:
Pooja Agarwal

Published by Ink of Knowledge
Sidhpur, Gujarat, India - 384151

ISBN: 978-93-5826-370-1

SKU: IOK305

Memory Miracle

Dr. Pooja Agarwal

PREFACE

Dr. Pooja Agarwal is a driven author with a keen interest in legal writing. Her remarkable success in various competitions and scholarly pursuits reflects her expertise in legal matters and her passion for the law. Having authored several books focused on legal topics, her works showcase a deep understanding of the law and the ability to articulate complex legal concepts clearly. Dr. Agarwal's exceptional legal acumen is evident through her victories in prestigious competitions such as the National Legislation and case commentary Drafting Competition. Her dedication and contributions to the legal field have garnered recognition from esteemed figures, with her paper being included in the book of Hon'ble J. Dipak Misra as a guide for aspiring legal professionals. As a top-performing student, Dr. Agarwal's thirst for knowledge and her passion for the law, exceptional writing abilities, and continuous pursuit of excellence indicate that she is destined for great success in her academic and professional journey, making her prominent figure in the legal community.

Dr. Pooja Agarwal

TABLE OF CONTENT

Chapter 1: Understanding Memory 5

- Introduction to memory and its importance
- Types of memory: short-term memory, long-term memory, sensory memory
- How memory works: encoding, storage, retrieval
- Factors affecting memory: age, health, environment, lifestyle

Chapter 2: Memory Improvement Techniques 12

- Memory enhancement strategies
- Mnemonics: memory aids and techniques
- Visualization and association techniques
- Chunking and organization methods
- Repetition and rehearsal techniques
- Mindfulness and meditation for memory improvement

Chapter 3: Memory Training Exercises 25

- Memory games and exercises
- Brain training apps and programs
- Memory challenges and puzzles
- Memory competitions and events
- Daily habits for memory improvement

Chapter 4: Enhancing Specific Types of Memory.... 37

- Improving short-term memory

Dr. Pooja Agarwal

- Strengthening long-term memory
- Enhancing episodic memory
- Boosting semantic memory
- Improving procedural memory

Chapter 5: Memory and Learning 48

- The relationship between memory and learning
- Effective study techniques for memory retention
- Retrieval practice and spaced repetition
- Creating optimal learning environments
- Applying memory techniques to academic and professional pursuits

Chapter 6: Memory in Daily Life 57

- Memory in personal and professional settings
- Remembering names and faces
- Improving memory for tasks and appointments
- Enhancing memory for speeches and presentations
- Memory strategies for daily activities and routines

Chapter 7: Memory and Aging 66

- Understanding age-related memory decline
- Strategies for maintaining memory function as you age
- Lifestyle factors that impact memory in older adults
- Memory exercises and activities for seniors
- Seeking professional help for memory concerns

Dr. Pooja Agarwal

Chapter 8: Memory Disorders and Conditions 73

- Common memory disorders: Alzheimer's disease, dementia, amnesia
- Causes and symptoms of memory disorders
- Diagnosis and treatment options
- Coping strategies for individuals and caregivers
- Research and advancements in memory disorder treatments

Chapter 9: Ethical Considerations in Memory Enhancement 81

- Ethical implications of memory enhancement technologies
- Privacy concerns in memory enhancement research
- Equity and access to memory enhancement resources
- Balancing memory enhancement with personal autonomy and identity

Chapter 10: Practical Applications of Memory Techniques 89

- Applying memory techniques in various fields
- Memory enhancement in education and training
- Memory techniques for professionals: educators, healthcare workers, public speakers
- Using memory techniques for personal growth and development

INTRODUCTION

Welcome to the captivating world of memory—an intricate and fascinating aspect of human cognition that shapes our experiences, influences our perceptions, and defines our identities. In this book, we embark on a journey to explore the mysteries of memory, unravel its complexities, and unlock its remarkable potential. Memory is more than just a repository of past experiences; it is the foundation of learning, the essence of identity, and the key to understanding the world around us. From the fleeting recollections of everyday life to the profound insights of historical events, memory serves as a bridge between the past, present, and future, connecting us to our personal narratives and collective histories. In the pages that follow, we will delve into the inner workings of memory, uncovering the cognitive processes that underlie its formation, storage, and retrieval. We will discover the various types of memory—short-term, long-term, sensory—and explore how they interact to shape our perceptions, thoughts, and behaviours. As we embark on this journey together, let us embrace the wonder of memory, celebrate its remarkable capabilities, and empower ourselves to harness its transformative power in our personal and professional endeavours. Together, we will unlock the secrets of memory and embark on a voyage of discovery through the extraordinary landscape of the human mind. Welcome to the world of memory—a realm where the past meets the present, and the possibilities are boundless.

Dr. Pooja Agarwal

Chapter 1: Understanding Memory

Introduction to Memory and Its Importance

Memory is a fundamental aspect of human cognition, enabling us to retain and recall information, experiences, and skills. It is the mental faculty that allows us to encode, store, and retrieve information over time. Without memory, our ability to learn, adapt, and function in the world would be severely impaired. Memory plays a crucial role in everyday activities, academic pursuits, professional endeavours, and personal relationships. Understanding memory is essential for enhancing cognitive abilities, optimizing learning processes, and maintaining cognitive health throughout life.

Types of Memory:

Memory is often classified into different types based on various factors such as duration, capacity, and sensory modalities. The three primary types of memory are:

1. Short-Term Memory (STM): *Short-term memory, also known as working memory, refers to the temporary storage and manipulation of information that is currently being used or processed. STM has limited capacity and duration, typically holding information for a few seconds to a minute. It plays a critical role in tasks requiring immediate attention, such as following instructions, solving problems, and making decisions.*

2. Long-Term Memory (LTM): *Long-term memory involves the storage of information over an extended period, ranging from minutes to years, or even a lifetime. LTM has a vast capacity and can store a wide range of information, including facts, events,* *experiences, and skills. It is subdivided into different types, including episodic memory (personal experiences), semantic memory (general knowledge), and procedural memory (skills and procedures).*

*3. **Sensory Memory:** Sensory memory is the brief retention of sensory impressions or stimuli from the environment. It acts as a buffer between sensory input and short-term memory, allowing us to perceive and process incoming information. Sensory memory is transient and holds information for a fraction of a second to a few seconds before either being forgotten or transferred to short-term memory for further processing.*

How Memory Works: Encoding, Storage, Retrieval

Memory involves a complex interplay of cognitive processes that enable the acquisition, retention, and retrieval of information. The process of memory can be divided into three stages:

1. Encoding: Encoding refers to the process of converting sensory input into a form that can be stored and processed by the brain. It involves transforming incoming information into neural codes or representations that can be stored in memory. Encoding strategies such as elaboration, repetition, and association play a crucial role in enhancing the effectiveness of encoding and improving memory retention.

2. Storage: Storage involves the retention of encoded information over time. Information is stored in different regions of the brain, with short-term memory relying on temporary activation of neural circuits, and long-term memory involving structural and functional changes in neuronal networks. Consolidation is the process by which memories are stabilized and strengthened over time, often occurring during sleep or periods of rest.

3. Retrieval: Retrieval is the process of accessing and bringing stored information back into consciousness. It involves reconstructing memories from stored traces and activating the neural networks associated with the encoded information. Retrieval cues, context, and familiarity can influence the ease and accuracy of memory retrieval. Techniques such as recall and recognition are used to retrieve information from memory.

Factors Affecting Memory: Age, Health, Environment, Lifestyle

Several factors can influence memory performance and cognitive function across the lifespan:

- Age: Memory abilities tend to decline with age, with older adults experiencing changes in

both short-term and long-term memory. However, age-related memory decline varies among individuals and can be influenced by genetic, lifestyle, and environmental factors.

- Health: Physical and mental health conditions, such as cardiovascular disease, diabetes, depression, and Alzheimer's disease, can impact memory function. Maintaining a healthy lifestyle, including regular exercise, balanced nutrition, adequate sleep, and stress management, can help preserve cognitive health and reduce the risk of memory disorders.

- Environment: Environmental factors, including education, socioeconomic status, social interactions, and cultural influences, can shape cognitive development and memory performance. Enriched environments that provide opportunities for learning, cognitive stimulation, and social engagement can promote cognitive resilience and memory functioning.

- Lifestyle: Lifestyle choices, such as cognitive engagement, intellectual activities, and lifelong learning, can contribute to cognitive vitality and memory preservation. Engaging in mentally stimulating activities, such as reading, puzzles, and hobbies, can help maintain cognitive function and support healthy aging.

In summary, understanding memory involves recognizing its various types, processes, and influencing factors. By gaining insights into how memory works and what factors affect its function, individuals can adopt strategies to enhance memory performance, optimize learning experiences, and promote cognitive well-being throughout life.

Chapter 2: Memory Improvement Techniques

Memory enhancement is a valuable skill that can be developed through various strategies and techniques. By employing effective memory improvement techniques, individuals can enhance their ability to encode, store, and retrieve information, leading to improved learning outcomes and cognitive performance.

Memory Enhancement Strategies

Memory enhancement strategies encompass a wide range of techniques aimed at optimizing memory function. These strategies involve adopting habits, utilizing tools, and practicing exercises that promote efficient information processing and retention. Some key memory enhancement strategies include:

1. Active Engagement: Actively engage with the material you wish to remember by paying attention, processing information deeply, and making meaningful connections. Actively engaging with the material increases the likelihood of encoding the information into long-term memory.

2. Organization: Organize information into logical structures, categories, or outlines to facilitate comprehension and retention. Creating mental frameworks or visual representations of information helps improve understanding and memory recall.

3. Retrieval Practice: Practice retrieving information from memory through regular self-testing or quizzes. Retrieval practice strengthens memory retrieval pathways and enhances long-term retention of information.

4. *Spaced Repetition: Space out review sessions over time to reinforce memory retention. Spaced repetition involves revisiting material at gradually increasing intervals, which enhances memory consolidation and prevents forgetting.*

5. *Multisensory Learning: Engage multiple sensory modalities, such as auditory, visual, and kinaesthetic, to enhance memory encoding and retrieval. Incorporating multisensory experiences into learning activities improves information processing and enhances memory consolidation.*

Mnemonics: Memory Aids and Techniques

Mnemonics are memory aids or techniques that facilitate the recall of information through the use of associations, acronyms, imagery, or patterns. Mnemonics leverage the brain's natural ability to remember vivid or meaningful cues, making it easier to retrieve stored information. Some popular mnemonic techniques include:

1. Acronyms: Create memorable acronyms or abbreviations by using the initial letters of a series of words or concepts. Acronyms help organize and recall information by providing a simple and memorable mnemonic device.

Example: HOMES to remember the names of the Great Lakes (Huron, Ontario, Michigan, Erie, Superior).

2. Visualization: Visualize vivid mental images or scenes that represent the information you want to remember. Visual imagery enhances memory encoding and retrieval by creating associations between visual cues and stored information.

Example: To remember a grocery list, visualize each item in a specific location within a familiar room or environment.

Dr. Pooja Agarwal

3. Method of Loci: Associate items or concepts with specific locations in a familiar mental or physical space, such as a house or neighbourhood. The method of loci relies on spatial memory and visualization to recall information in a sequential order.

Example: To remember a speech outline, mentally associate key points with different rooms in a familiar house.

Visualization and Association Techniques

Visualization and association techniques involve mentally linking new information with existing knowledge or creating visual representations to aid memory retention. These techniques leverage the brain's capacity for visual processing and associative learning to enhance memory encoding and recall. Some effective visualization and association techniques include:

1. Memory Palaces: Create imaginary spatial environments, such as palaces, landscapes, or rooms, to store and organize information. Use vivid imagery and spatial associations to mentally place items or concepts within the memory palace for easy retrieval.

Example: To memorize a list of historical dates, imagine walking through a grand palace and associating each date with a distinct location or object within the palace.

2. Keyword Method: Associate new vocabulary words or concepts with familiar keywords or phrases that sound similar or have related meanings. Use vivid mental images or word associations to link the keyword with the target information.

Example: To remember the Spanish word "zapato" (shoe), associate it with the English word "zap" and visualize a shoe getting zapped by electricity.

Dr. Pooja Agarwal

Chunking and Organization Methods

Chunking and organization methods involve breaking down large amounts of information into smaller, more manageable units or categories. By organizing information into meaningful chunks or categories, individuals can improve memory encoding, retention, and retrieval. Some effective chunking and organization methods include:

1. Grouping: Group related items or concepts together based on common attributes, themes, or categories. Organizing information into meaningful groups reduces cognitive load and enhances memory organization and recall.

Example: Grouping animals into categories such as mammals, birds, reptiles, and amphibians.

2. Hierarchical Structure: Create hierarchical structures or frameworks to organize information in a nested format, with broader categories encompassing subcategories or specific details. Hierarchical organization facilitates comprehension and memory retrieval by establishing relationships between concepts.

Example: Organizing a list of plants into categories such as trees, shrubs, flowers, and grasses, with subcategories for each type.

Repetition and Rehearsal Techniques

Repetition and rehearsal techniques involve repeatedly reviewing and practicing information to reinforce memory retention and recall. By engaging in deliberate rehearsal and spaced repetition, individuals can strengthen memory traces and improve long-term retention. Some effective repetition and rehearsal techniques include:

1. Spaced Repetition: Distribute study sessions over time and gradually increase the intervals between review sessions. Spaced repetition optimizes memory consolidation and enhances long-term retention by leveraging the spacing effect.

2. Active Recall: Practice actively retrieving information from memory through self-testing or recall exercises. Actively recalling information strengthens memory retrieval pathways and promotes deeper encoding of information.

3. Distributed Practice: Break study sessions into shorter, more frequent intervals spaced out over time. Distributed practice enhances memory consolidation and reduces the risk of cognitive fatigue or overload.

Mindfulness and Meditation for Memory Improvement

Mindfulness and meditation practices can enhance memory function by promoting focused attention, cognitive clarity, and emotional regulation. Mindfulness techniques cultivate present-moment awareness and nonjudgmental acceptance, which can improve memory encoding, retrieval, and retention. Some mindfulness and meditation practices for memory improvement include:

1. Mindful Awareness: Cultivate mindful awareness of sensory experiences, thoughts, and emotions during learning and memory tasks. Pay attention to the present moment and maintain focused awareness on the information being processed.

2. Concentration Meditation: Practice concentration meditation techniques, such as focused attention on the breath or a specific object, to enhance concentration and attentional control. Concentration meditation strengthens cognitive abilities that support memory encoding and retrieval.

3. Loving-Kindness Meditation: Engage in loving-kindness meditation practices to cultivate positive emotions, empathy, and compassion. Loving-kindness meditation promotes emotional well-being and reduces stress, which can enhance memory performance and cognitive function.

Memory Improvement Techniques

Visual representations can aid in understanding and implementing memory improvement techniques effectively. Below are illustrated examples of mnemonic devices, visualization techniques, chunking methods, and mindfulness practices for memory enhancement:

Dr. Pooja Agarwal

- Mnemonic Devices: Illustration of acronyms, visualization techniques, and keyword associations used to memorize lists, vocabulary, and sequences.

- Visualization Techniques: Visual representations of memory palaces, method of loci, and spatial associations for organizing and recalling information.

- Chunking Methods: Graphic representations of grouping strategies, hierarchical structures, and categorization techniques for organizing complex information.

- Mindfulness Practices: Illustrations of mindfulness exercises, concentration meditation techniques, and loving-kindness meditation practices for enhancing memory function and cognitive well-being.

Incorporating visual aids and illustrations can enhance comprehension, retention, and application of memory improvement techniques. By integrating visual representations with practical exercises and strategies, individuals can optimize their memory performance and cognitive abilities effectively.

Chapter 3: Memory Training Exercises

Memory training exercises are essential tools for improving cognitive function, enhancing memory capacity, and maintaining mental agility. These exercises engage various aspects of memory, including recall, recognition, and associative learning, while providing opportunities for mental stimulation and growth. By incorporating memory training exercises into daily routines, individuals can sharpen their cognitive skills and optimize their memory performance.

Memory Games and Exercises

Memory games and exercises offer entertaining and interactive ways to challenge and improve memory function. These activities stimulate different cognitive processes, such as attention, concentration, and pattern recognition, while providing enjoyable mental stimulation. Some popular memory games and exercises include:

1. Card Matching: Match pairs of cards with identical images or symbols by flipping them over one at a time. Card matching games enhance visual memory, attention, and spatial awareness.

2. Concentration: Arrange a set of cards facedown and take turns flipping over two cards at a time to find matching pairs. Concentration games require focused attention, visual scanning, and memory recall.

3. Word Recall: Create a list of words or phrases and study them for a set period. Then, try to recall as many words as possible from the list without referring back to it. Word recall exercises strengthen verbal memory and retrieval skills.

Dr. Pooja Agarwal

4. Number Sequences: Memorize and reproduce sequences of numbers or symbols in ascending or descending order. Number sequence exercises enhance working memory, attention to detail, and mental flexibility.

Brain Training Apps and Programs

Brain training apps and programs offer a convenient and accessible way to engage in structured memory exercises and cognitive challenges. These digital platforms provide a variety of games, puzzles, and activities designed to target specific cognitive functions and promote mental fitness. Some popular brain training apps and programs include:

1. Lumosity: Lumosity offers a collection of brain training games and activities designed to improve memory, attention, problem-solving, and cognitive flexibility.

2. *Peak: Peak features personalized brain training programs that adapt to individual skill levels and preferences. It offers a wide range of games and challenges to target memory, language, and mental agility.*

3. *Elevate: Elevate provides daily brain training workouts focusing on critical cognitive skills, including memory, processing speed, and comprehension. It offers personalized training programs tailored to individual performance and goals.*

4. *CogniFit: CogniFit offers scientifically validated cognitive assessments and personalized training programs to improve memory, attention, and other cognitive abilities. It provides a comprehensive approach to cognitive enhancement through engaging activities and progress tracking.*

Memory Challenges and Puzzles

Memory challenges and puzzles offer stimulating and challenging exercises to test and improve memory function. These activities require strategic thinking, problem-solving skills, and memory recall abilities. Some popular memory challenges and puzzles include:

1. Sudoku: Sudoku puzzles involve filling a grid with numbers based on specific rules and patterns. Solving Sudoku puzzles requires logical reasoning, pattern recognition, and memory recall skills.

2. Crossword Puzzles: Crossword puzzles involve filling in words based on intersecting clues provided in a grid. Solving crossword puzzles requires vocabulary knowledge, memory retrieval, and problem-solving abilities.

3. *Memory Match: Memory match puzzles feature a grid of facedown cards that players must flip over to find matching pairs. Memory match puzzles challenge visual memory, attention, and concentration skills.*

4. *Jigsaw Puzzles: Jigsaw puzzles involve assembling pieces to form a complete picture or image. Solving jigsaw puzzles requires spatial reasoning, visual memory, and problem-solving abilities.*

Memory Competitions and Events

Memory competitions and events provide opportunities for individuals to showcase their memory skills, compete against others, and engage in friendly competition. These events feature a variety of memory challenges, tasks, and disciplines designed to test different aspects of memory function. Some common memory competitions and events include:

1. Memory Championships: Memory championships involve competitive events where participants compete in various memory tasks, such as memorizing decks of cards, strings of numbers, and lists of words.

2. Memory Tournaments: Memory tournaments feature head-to-head competitions where participants compete in timed memory challenges, rapid recall tasks, and memory-based games.

3. Memory Leagues: Memory leagues offer organized competitions and leagues where individuals or teams compete in regular matches, tournaments, and events throughout the season.

4. Memory Clubs and Societies: Memory clubs and societies provide forums for memory enthusiasts to meet, share techniques, and participate in informal competitions, workshops, and training sessions.

Daily Habits for Memory Improvement

In addition to structured memory exercises and challenges, cultivating daily habits that promote cognitive health and memory improvement is essential. Incorporating simple lifestyle practices and behaviours into daily routines can contribute to long-term cognitive vitality and mental well-being. Some daily habits for memory improvement include:

1. Physical Exercise: Engage in regular physical exercise, such as brisk walking, jogging, cycling, or yoga, to improve blood flow to the brain, reduce stress, and enhance cognitive function.

2. Healthy Diet: Maintain balanced and nutritious diet rich in fruits, vegetables, whole grains, lean proteins, and omega-3 fatty acids to support brain health and cognitive function.

3. Mental Stimulation: Challenge your brain with intellectually stimulating activities, such as reading, puzzles, games, learning new skills, or pursuing hobbies and interests.

4. Adequate Sleep: Prioritize quality sleep by establishing a consistent sleep schedule, creating a relaxing bedtime routine, and ensuring a comfortable sleep environment. Adequate sleep is essential for memory consolidation, cognitive processing, and overall brain health.

5. Stress Management: Practice stress-reduction techniques, such as deep breathing, meditation, mindfulness, and relaxation exercises, to alleviate stress and promote mental clarity and focus.

Memory Training Exercises

Illustrated examples of memory training exercises, brain training apps, memory challenges, and daily habits for memory improvement:

- Memory Games: Visual representations of card matching, concentration, word recall, and number sequence games to enhance memory function.

- Brain Training Apps: Illustrations of popular brain training apps, such as Lumosity, Peak, Elevate, and CogniFit, offering personalized cognitive workouts and challenges.

Dr. Pooja Agarwal

- Memory Puzzles: Graphic representations of Sudoku, crossword puzzles, memory match, and jigsaw puzzles to stimulate memory recall and problem-solving skills.

- Memory Competitions: Visual depictions of memory championships, tournaments, leagues, and clubs where participants engage in competitive memory challenges and events.

- Daily Habits: Illustrated examples of physical exercise, healthy diet, mental stimulation, adequate sleep, and stress management techniques for promoting cognitive health and memory improvement.

Incorporating illustrated examples and practical exercises into memory training programs enhances engagement, comprehension, and retention of memory enhancement techniques. By integrating diverse memory training exercises and habits into daily routines, individuals can cultivate cognitive resilience, optimize memory performance, and support overall brain health and well-being.

Chapter 4: Enhancing Specific Types of Memory

Memory is a multifaceted cognitive function that encompasses various types and processes. Each type of memory serves unique functions and relies on distinct neural mechanisms. By understanding the specific characteristics and requirements of different types of memory, individuals can implement targeted strategies and techniques to enhance their memory performance effectively.

Improving Short-Term Memory

Short-term memory, also known as working memory, is responsible for temporarily holding and manipulating information for immediate use. It plays a crucial role in tasks requiring attention, concentration, and problem-solving. To improve short-term memory, individuals can employ the following strategies:

1. Chunking: Grouping related items or information into smaller, more manageable chunks can enhance short-term memory capacity and retention. By organizing information into meaningful clusters, individuals can reduce cognitive load and facilitate easier recall.

2. Visualization: Visualizing mental images or spatial arrangements associated with the information being processed can aid short-term memory encoding and retention. Creating vivid mental images helps make abstract or complex information more tangible and memorable.

3. Repetition: Repeating information aloud or silently to oneself can reinforce short-term memory retention and prevent forgetting.

Repetition strengthens memory traces and enhances the stability of information stored in short-term memory.

4. *Mnemonics: Employing mnemonic devices, such as acronyms, rhymes, or visual associations, can help encode and retain information in short-term memory more effectively. Mnemonics provide memorable cues or aids that facilitate the retrieval of stored information.*

Strengthening Long-Term Memory

Long-term memory involves the encoding, storage, and retrieval of information over extended periods, ranging from minutes to years. Long-term memory encompasses various subtypes, including episodic memory, semantic memory, and procedural memory. To strengthen long-term memory, individuals can implement the following strategies:

1. Elaborative Encoding: Engaging in deeper levels of processing by connecting new information with existing knowledge or personal experiences enhances long-term memory retention. Elaborative encoding involves making meaningful associations and integrating new information into existing cognitive frameworks.

2. Spaced Repetition: Distributing study or practice sessions over time and spacing out review sessions enhances long-term memory consolidation and retention. Spaced repetition leverages the spacing effect, which suggests that information is better retained when reviewed at intervals rather than in a single session.

3. Retrieval Practice: Actively retrieving information from memory through self-testing, quizzes, or recall exercises strengthens long-term memory retrieval pathways and promotes durable learning. Retrieval practice enhances memory consolidation and fosters deeper encoding of information.

4. Contextual Learning: Providing context-rich environments or incorporating multisensory experiences during learning enhances long-term memory encoding and retrieval. Contextual learning facilitates the formation of rich memory traces by associating information with sensory cues, emotions, and environmental cues.

Enhancing Episodic Memory

Episodic memory involves the recollection of personal experiences, events, and autobiographical details tied to specific times and places. Enhancing episodic memory involves strategies that promote detailed encoding, vivid retrieval cues, and contextual associations. To boost episodic memory, individuals can implement the following techniques:

1. Narrative Storytelling: Constructing narratives or stories around personal experiences helps organize episodic memories into coherent and meaningful sequences. Narrative storytelling provides a framework for encoding and recalling episodic details in chronological order.

2. Visual Imagery: Visualizing vivid mental images or scenes associated with episodic memories enhances encoding and retrieval of autobiographical details. Visual imagery helps make episodic memories more salient and memorable by providing sensory-rich cues.

3. Sensory Reminiscence: Engaging sensory modalities, such as sight, sound, smell, taste, and touch, associated with past experiences

enhances episodic memory retrieval. Sensory reminiscence evokes multisensory cues that trigger vivid recollections of specific events or moments.

Boosting Semantic Memory

Semantic memory encompasses general knowledge, facts, concepts, and vocabulary stored in long-term memory. Enhancing semantic memory involves strategies that promote meaningful encoding, semantic organization, and retrieval fluency. To boost semantic memory, individuals can utilize the following techniques:

1. Semantic Mapping: Creating semantic maps or concept webs that visually represent relationships between related concepts and categories enhances semantic memory organization and retrieval. Semantic mapping helps identify hierarchical structures and associative links within semantic networks.

2. Semantic Elaboration: Elaborating on semantic concepts by generating examples, analogies, or explanations promotes deeper encoding and retention of semantic knowledge. Semantic elaboration involves connecting new information with existing semantic networks and establishing meaningful associations.

3. Semantic Retrieval Practice: Practicing semantic retrieval tasks, such as category fluency tests or semantic associations, strengthens semantic memory retrieval pathways and improves retrieval fluency. Semantic retrieval practice enhances access to stored knowledge and promotes flexible thinking.

Improving Procedural Memory

Procedural memory involves the acquisition and execution of motor skills, habits, and procedural routines through repeated practice and reinforcement. Enhancing procedural memory requires systematic practice, skill refinement, and feedback-driven learning. To improve procedural memory, individuals can implement the following strategies:

1. Deliberate Practice: Engaging in deliberate, focused practice sessions that target specific procedural skills and techniques fosters skill acquisition and procedural memory consolidation. Deliberate practice involves breaking down complex tasks into manageable components and gradually increasing difficulty levels.

2. Skill Chunking: Breaking down procedural tasks into smaller, more manageable chunks or sequences enhances procedural memory encoding and execution. Skill chunking involves grouping related actions or movements into cohesive patterns that can be executed efficiently.

3. *Feedback and Error Correction:* Providing timely and constructive feedback during practice sessions helps identify areas for improvement and facilitates procedural memory refinement. Feedback-driven learning involves recognizing errors, adjusting performance strategies, and reinforcing successful execution.

4. *Repetition and Reinforcement:* Repetition and reinforcement of procedural tasks through consistent practice and reinforcement strengthen procedural memory traces and automate skill execution. Repetitive practice promotes procedural fluency and

automaticity, enabling smoother and more efficient task performance.

Incorporating targeted strategies and techniques for enhancing specific types of memory can optimize memory performance, promote cognitive flexibility, and support lifelong learning. By understanding the unique characteristics and requirements of different memory systems, individuals can develop personalized memory enhancement routines tailored to their cognitive strengths and learning objectives.

Chapter 5: Memory and Learning

Memory and learning are intricately interconnected processes that play vital roles in acquiring, retaining, and utilizing information effectively. Understanding the relationship between memory and learning is essential for developing efficient study techniques, optimizing learning outcomes, and enhancing cognitive performance across various academic and professional domains.

The Relationship between Memory and Learning

Memory and learning are complementary processes that mutually influence and support each other. Learning involves the acquisition of new knowledge, skills, and concepts, while memory encompasses the encoding, storage, and retrieval of learned information over time. Memory serves as the foundation for learning by allowing individuals to retain and recall information acquired through educational experiences, practice, and exposure to new stimuli. Conversely, learning enriches memory by providing meaningful contexts, associations, and connections that enhance memory encoding and consolidation. The dynamic interaction between memory and learning facilitates the development of expertise, problem-solving abilities, and adaptive behaviours essential for academic success and lifelong learning.

Effective Study Techniques for Memory Retention

Effective study techniques are essential for maximizing memory retention, comprehension, and recall of learned material. By employing evidence-based study strategies and cognitive principles, individuals can optimize their learning experiences and improve memory performance. Some effective study techniques for memory retention include:

1. Active Engagement: Actively engage with the material by asking questions, summarizing key concepts, and making connections to prior knowledge. Active learning promotes deeper understanding and enhances memory encoding.

2. Elaborative Rehearsal: Elaborate on the material by generating examples, analogies, and explanations that relate to real-world contexts. Elaborative rehearsal involves making meaningful associations and integrating new information with existing knowledge structures.

3. Distributed Practice: Distribute study sessions over time and space out review sessions to promote memory consolidation and retention. Spacing out practice sessions

enhances long-term memory retention and reduces the risk of forgetting.

4. Interleaved Practice: Interleave different topics or subjects within study sessions to promote cognitive flexibility and enhance memory retrieval. Interleaved practice involves alternating between different types of material to reinforce learning and prevent interference.

Retrieval Practice and Spaced Repetition

Retrieval practice and spaced repetition are powerful memory enhancement techniques that leverage principles of memory consolidation, retrieval fluency, and distributed practice. Retrieval practice involves actively recalling information from memory through self-testing, quizzes, and recall exercises. Spaced repetition entails spacing out review sessions over increasing intervals to reinforce memory retention and promote long-term learning. By integrating retrieval practice and spaced repetition into study routines, individuals can enhance memory consolidation, strengthen memory retrieval pathways, and improve learning efficiency.

Creating Optimal Learning Environments

Creating optimal learning environments is essential for fostering concentration, motivation, and engagement, which are critical factors for effective learning and memory retention. Optimal learning environments should be conducive to active learning, collaboration, and exploration while minimizing distractions and disruptions. Some strategies for creating optimal learning environments include:

1. Minimize Distractions: Eliminate or minimize distractions, such as noise, clutter, and interruptions, to promote focused attention and concentration during study sessions.

2. Establish a Routine: Establish a consistent study routine and dedicated study space that signals the brain to focus and engage in learning activities.

3. Utilize Technology Wisely: Use technology strategically to support learning goals and minimize distractions. Utilize digital tools, such as productivity apps, note-taking software, and online resources, to enhance organization, efficiency, and accessibility of study materials.

4. Incorporate Active Learning Strategies: Incorporate active learning strategies, such as group discussions, problem-solving activities, and hands-on experiments, to promote engagement, collaboration, and deeper understanding of course material.

Applying Memory Techniques to Academic and Professional Pursuits

Applying memory techniques to academic and professional pursuits can enhance learning efficiency, productivity, and performance across diverse domains. By incorporating memory-enhancing strategies and techniques into study routines, individuals can optimize their cognitive resources, overcome learning challenges, and achieve academic and professional goals more effectively. Some ways to apply memory techniques to academic and professional pursuits include:

1. Mnemonics and Memory Aids: Use mnemonic devices, memory aids, and visualization techniques to memorize complex information, formulas, and concepts in academic subjects and professional contexts.

2. Concept Mapping and Visualization: Create concept maps, diagrams, and visual representations to organize and connect related ideas, theories, and principles. Concept mapping enhances comprehension, facilitates memory encoding, and promotes critical thinking skills.

3. Reflective Practice: Engage in reflective practice by reviewing and analyzing past learning experiences, identifying strengths and areas for improvement, and setting goals for future learning and professional development. Reflective practice fosters metacognitive awareness, self-regulation, and lifelong learning habits.

4. Collaborative Learning: Participate in collaborative learning activities, such as study groups, peer tutoring, and team projects, to exchange ideas, share perspectives, and deepen understanding of course material. Collaborative learning promotes social interaction, collective problem-solving, and knowledge construction in academic and professional settings.

By understanding the dynamic interplay between memory and learning processes, individuals can adopt effective study techniques, leverage memory enhancement strategies, and create optimal learning environments to maximize learning outcomes and achieve academic and professional success.

Chapter 6: Memory in Daily Life

Memory plays a pivotal role in our daily lives, influencing our interactions, productivity, and overall well-being in both personal and professional settings. From remembering names and faces to recalling important tasks and appointments, memory is essential for navigating daily activities and routines effectively. By understanding memory processes and employing memory enhancement techniques, individuals can optimize their cognitive function and improve memory performance in various aspects of daily life.

Memory in Personal and Professional Settings

Memory is integral to personal and professional interactions, communication, and decision-making processes. In personal settings, memory allows us to recall cherished moments, experiences, and relationships, fostering emotional connections and interpersonal bonds. In professional settings, memory enables us to retain and apply knowledge, skills, and information relevant to our work responsibilities and goals. Memory facilitates learning, problem-solving, and adaptation to new challenges, enhancing productivity and effectiveness in professional endeavours.

Remembering Names and Faces

Remembering names and faces is a common memory challenge faced in social and professional situations. Effective strategies for remembering names and faces include:

1. Active Listening: Pay close attention and actively listen when introduced to someone, repeating their name mentally or aloud to reinforce memory encoding.

2. *Association:* Associate the person's name with distinctive facial features, physical attributes, or memorable characteristics to create meaningful connections and aid recall.

3. *Repetition:* Repeat the person's name during conversation and use it in context to reinforce memory retrieval and familiarity.

4. *Visualization:* Visualize the person's face and name together, creating mental images or stories that link the two elements for easier recall.

Improving Memory for Tasks and Appointments

Dr. Pooja Agarwal

Improving memory for tasks and appointments is crucial for staying organized, productive, and on schedule. Some strategies for enhancing memory for tasks and appointments include:

1. Use of Reminders: Utilize digital calendars, task management apps, and alarms to set reminders for important deadlines, meetings, and appointments.

2. Prioritization: Prioritize tasks and appointments based on urgency, importance, and deadlines, allocating time and resources accordingly.

3. Break Tasks into Smaller Steps: Break down complex tasks into smaller, manageable steps or milestones, making it easier to track progress and complete tasks efficiently.

4. Visual Aids: Use visual aids, such as to-do lists, checklists, and calendars, to visually represent tasks, deadlines, and appointments, enhancing memory retention and organization.

Enhancing Memory for Speeches and Presentations

Enhancing memory for speeches and presentations is essential for effective communication and public speaking. Strategies for improving memory for speeches and presentations include:

1. Structured Outlines: Create structured outlines or frameworks that organize key points, themes, and supporting details in a logical sequence, aiding memory retrieval and organization.

2. Practice and Rehearsal: Practice delivering speeches and presentations multiple times, focusing on memorizing key points, transitions, and visual aids to enhance fluency and confidence.

3. Visualization Techniques: Visualize the flow of the speech or presentation, mentally rehearsing each segment and visualizing the audience's positive response and engagement.

4. Mnemonics and Memory Aids: Use mnemonic devices, memory aids, and acronyms to remember key points, anecdotes, or statistical data, enhancing memory retention and recall during delivery.

Memory Strategies for Daily Activities and Routines

Incorporating memory strategies into daily activities and routines can improve efficiency, productivity, and organization. Some memory strategies for daily life include:

1. Establishing Routines: Establish consistent routines and habits for daily activities, such as meal planning, exercise, and sleep schedules, reducing cognitive load and enhancing memory retention.

2. Utilizing External Aids: Use external aids, such as sticky notes, planners, and digital reminders, to help remember tasks, errands, and appointments, reducing reliance on memory alone.

3. Mental Rehearsal: Mentally rehearse upcoming tasks, activities, or conversations, visualizing the steps involved and anticipating potential challenges or obstacles.

4. Review and Reflection: Take time to review and reflect on daily experiences, accomplishments, and lessons learned, consolidating memory traces and promoting continuous improvement and self-awareness.

Memory in Daily Life

Visual representations of memory in daily life, including:

- Remembering Names and Faces: Illustration of strategies for remembering names and faces, such as active listening, association, repetition, and visualization.

- Improving Memory for Tasks and Appointments: Graphic representation of memory enhancement strategies for tasks and appointments, including the use of reminders, prioritization, task breakdowns, and visual aids.

- *Enhancing Memory for Speeches and Presentations: Visual depiction of memory strategies for speeches and presentations, such as structured outlines, practice and rehearsal, visualization techniques, and mnemonic devices.*

- *Memory Strategies for Daily Activities and Routines: Illustration of memory strategies for daily life, including establishing routines, utilizing external aids, mental rehearsal, and review and reflection.*

By implementing memory enhancement techniques and strategies into daily routines and activities, individuals can optimize memory performance, increase productivity, and enhance overall cognitive function in personal and professional contexts.

Chapter 7: Memory and Aging

Memory and aging are closely intertwined, as individuals may experience changes in memory function as they grow older. Understanding age-related memory decline, adopting strategies for maintaining memory function, considering lifestyle factors, engaging in memory exercises, and seeking professional help are essential aspects of addressing memory concerns in older adults.

Understanding Age-Related Memory Decline

Age-related memory decline refers to changes in memory function that occur naturally as individuals age. While some degree of memory decline is a normal part of the aging process, severe or progressive memory impairments may indicate underlying cognitive disorders, such as Alzheimer's disease or other forms of dementia. Age-related memory decline may manifest in various ways, including:

1. Slower Processing Speed: Older adults may experience slower cognitive processing speed, making it take longer to encode, retrieve, or manipulate information.

2. Reduced Working Memory Capacity: Working memory capacity, which is responsible for temporarily holding and manipulating information, may decline with age, affecting multitasking and complex cognitive tasks.

3. Difficulty with Episodic Memory: Episodic memory, which involves recalling specific events and personal experiences, may become less efficient with age, leading to difficulties remembering recent events or details.

4. Tip-of-the-Tongue Phenomenon: Older adults may experience the tip-of-the-tongue phenomenon more frequently, where they struggle to recall a word or name despite knowing it's stored in memory.

Strategies for Maintaining Memory Function as You Age

While age-related memory decline is natural, there are strategies that older adults can adopt to maintain cognitive function and mitigate memory impairment:

1. Mental Stimulation: Engage in mentally stimulating activities, such as reading, puzzles, crossword puzzles, and learning new skills, to keep the brain active and engaged.

2. Social Engagement: Maintain social connections and engage in social activities, clubs, and groups to foster social interaction, emotional support, and cognitive stimulation.

Dr. Pooja Agarwal

3. Physical Exercise: Regular physical exercise, including aerobic exercise, strength training, and balance exercises, can improve blood flow to the brain, reduce the risk of cognitive decline, and enhance overall brain health.

4. Healthy Diet: Follow balanced and nutritious diet rich in fruits, vegetables, whole grains, lean proteins, and omega-3 fatty acids to support brain health and cognitive function.

Lifestyle Factors That Impact Memory in Older Adults

Several lifestyle factors can impact memory function in older adults:

1. Sleep Quality: Poor sleep quality or insufficient sleep can impair memory consolidation and cognitive function. Maintain a regular sleep schedule and practice good sleep hygiene habits to promote restful sleep.

2. *Stress Management:* Chronic stress can negatively impact memory function and cognitive performance. Practice stress-reduction techniques, such as mindfulness, meditation, deep breathing exercises, and relaxation techniques.

3. *Substance Use:* Avoid excessive alcohol consumption and illicit drug use, as they can impair memory function and cognitive abilities.

Memory Exercises and Activities for Seniors

Engaging in memory exercises and activities can help older adults maintain cognitive function and enhance memory performance:

1. Word Games and Puzzles: Play word games, crossword puzzles, Sudoku, and other brain-training activities to challenge memory, attention, and problem-solving skills.

2. Memory Journals: Keep a memory journal or diary to document daily experiences, events, and reflections, promoting memory consolidation and self-awareness.

3. Reminiscence Therapy: Engage in reminiscence therapy activities, such as storytelling, photo albums, and memory prompts, to evoke positive memories and stimulate cognitive function.

Seeking Professional Help for Memory Concerns

If memory concerns persist or worsen over time, it is important for older adults to seek professional help from healthcare providers, such as primary care physicians, neurologists, or geriatric specialists. Professional evaluation and diagnosis can help identify underlying causes of memory impairment and guide appropriate treatment and management strategies. Early intervention and proactive management of memory concerns can help optimize cognitive function, enhance quality of life, and support overall well-being in older adults.

In summary, understanding age-related memory decline, adopting strategies for maintaining memory function, considering lifestyle factors, engaging in memory exercises, and seeking professional help are crucial aspects of addressing memory concerns in older adults. By taking proactive steps to support cognitive health and well-being, older adults can maintain independence, vitality, and a high quality of life as they age.

Dr. Pooja Agarwal

Chapter 8: Memory Disorders and Conditions

Memory disorders and conditions encompass a range of neurological conditions that affect memory function and cognitive abilities. Understanding common memory disorders, their causes, symptoms, diagnosis, treatment options, coping strategies for individuals and caregivers, as well as ongoing research and advancements in treatment, is essential for addressing the challenges associated with these conditions.

Common Memory Disorders

1. Alzheimer's Disease: Alzheimer's disease is a progressive neurodegenerative disorder characterized by a decline in memory, cognition, and functional abilities. It is the most common cause of dementia in older adults and is characterized by the accumulation of abnormal proteins in the brain, including beta-amyloid plaques and tau tangles.

2. Dementia: Dementia is a syndrome characterized by a decline in cognitive function, including memory, language, problem-solving, and judgment, severe enough to interfere with daily activities. Alzheimer's disease is the most common cause of dementia, but other causes include vascular dementia, Lewy body dementia, and frontotemporal dementia.

3. Amnesia: Amnesia refers to a partial or complete loss of memory, typically resulting from brain injury, trauma, stroke, or neurological conditions. It can affect short-term or long-term memory and may be temporary or permanent, depending on the underlying cause.

Dr. Pooja Agarwal

Causes and Symptoms of Memory Disorders

Memory disorders can have various causes, including genetic predisposition, brain injury, neurodegenerative processes, vascular factors, and environmental influences. The symptoms of memory disorders vary depending on the underlying condition but may include:

- Progressive memory loss

- Confusion and disorientation

-   Difficulty   with   language   and communication

- Impaired judgment and reasoning

- Changes in mood and behaviour

- Disruption of daily activities and routines

Diagnosis and Treatment Options

Diagnosis of memory disorders involves a comprehensive evaluation, including medical history, physical examination, neurological assessments, cognitive testing, imaging studies (such as MRI or CT scans), and laboratory tests. Treatment options for memory disorders depend on the underlying cause and may include:

- Medications: Medications such as cholinesterase inhibitors and memantine may be prescribed to manage symptoms and slow the progression of memory disorders, particularly in Alzheimer's disease.

- Cognitive Rehabilitation: Cognitive rehabilitation programs may help individuals with memory disorders learn compensatory strategies, improve cognitive function, and enhance quality of life.

- Lifestyle Modifications: Adopting a healthy lifestyle, including regular exercise, a balanced diet, social engagement, and mental stimulation, may help support brain health and cognitive function.

- *Supportive Care: Providing support and assistance with daily activities, safety measures, and emotional support is essential for individuals living with memory disorders and their caregivers.*

Coping Strategies for Individuals and Caregivers

Coping with memory disorders can be challenging for both individuals and their caregivers. Some coping strategies include:

- *Establishing Routines: Establishing consistent routines and schedules can help individuals with memory disorders feel more organized and secure.*

- *Simplifying Tasks: Breaking tasks down into smaller, manageable steps and providing clear instructions can help individuals with memory disorders maintain independence and confidence.*

- Seeking Support: Joining support groups, seeking counselling, and connecting with other individuals and families affected by memory disorders can provide emotional support and practical guidance.

- Respite Care: Taking breaks and seeking respite care services can help caregivers prevent burnout and maintain their own physical and emotional well-being.

Research and Advancements in Memory Disorder Treatments

Ongoing research and advancements in memory disorder treatments aim to improve early detection, develop disease-modifying therapies, and enhance quality of life for individuals affected by memory disorders. Areas of research include:

- Biomarker Discovery: Identifying biomarkers, such as protein levels in the blood or cerebrospinal fluid, imaging markers, and

genetic markers, may help improve early diagnosis and monitoring of memory disorders.

- Drug Development: Developing novel therapeutics, including disease-modifying drugs, immunotherapies, and gene therapies, is a focus of research to target underlying disease mechanisms and slow the progression of memory disorders.

- Non-Pharmacological Interventions: Investigating non-pharmacological interventions, such as lifestyle modifications, cognitive training programs, and brain stimulation techniques, may offer alternative or adjunctive approaches to managing memory disorders.

By advancing our understanding of memory disorders, promoting early detection and diagnosis, exploring innovative treatment approaches, and providing comprehensive support and care for individuals and families affected by memory disorders, we can work towards improving outcomes and enhancing quality of life for those impacted by these conditions.

Chapter 9: Ethical Considerations in Memory Enhancement

As advancements in neuroscience and technology continue to expand the possibilities for memory enhancement, it becomes increasingly important to address the ethical implications associated with these developments. Ethical considerations play a crucial role in guiding the responsible development, use, and dissemination of memory enhancement technologies. This chapter explores key ethical issues, including privacy concerns, equity and access, and the balance between memory enhancement and personal autonomy.

Ethical Implications of Memory Enhancement Technologies

Memory enhancement technologies hold the potential to improve cognitive function, *enhance learning, and alleviate memory-related impairments. However, ethical concerns arise regarding the unintended consequences and societal implications of these interventions. Some ethical considerations include:*

1. Safety and Efficacy: Ensuring the safety and efficacy of memory enhancement interventions is paramount to protect individuals from potential harm and exploitation. Rigorous research, clinical trials, and regulatory oversight are essential to evaluate the risks and benefits of these technologies.

2. Informed Consent: Respecting individuals' autonomy and right to self-determination requires obtaining informed consent before administering memory enhancement interventions. Individuals should be fully informed about the nature of the intervention, potential risks, and alternatives to make autonomous decisions about their participation.

3. Enhancement vs. Treatment: Distinguishing between memory enhancement for cognitive enhancement purposes and memory enhancement for therapeutic purposes is essential for ethical decision-making. While therapeutic interventions aim to alleviate memory impairments and improve quality of life, cognitive enhancement interventions raise questions about fairness, social justice, and the pursuit of perfection.

Privacy Concerns in Memory Enhancement Research

Memory enhancement research often involves the collection, storage, and analysis of sensitive personal data, raising significant privacy concerns. Privacy safeguards and ethical guidelines are necessary to protect individuals' privacy rights and prevent unauthorized access, misuse, or exploitation of their personal information. Some privacy considerations include:

1. Data Security: Implementing robust data security measures, encryption protocols, and access controls to safeguard personal data from unauthorized access, breaches, or cyber-attacks.

2. Anonymization and De-identification: Anonymizing or de-identifying personal data to remove identifiable information and protect individuals' privacy while facilitating data sharing and analysis for research purposes.

3. Transparency and Accountability: Promoting transparency and accountability in memory enhancement research by disclosing data handling practices, privacy policies, and potential risks associated with data collection and storage.

Equity and Access to Memory Enhancement Resources

Ensuring equitable access to memory enhancement resources is essential to promote fairness, social justice, and equal opportunities for all individuals. However, disparities in access to healthcare, education, and resources may exacerbate existing inequalities and perpetuate social stratification. Some considerations for promoting equity and access include:

1. Affordability and Accessibility: Making memory enhancement interventions, technologies, and services affordable, accessible, and available to marginalized and underserved populations, including low-

income individuals, racial and ethnic minorities, and individuals with disabilities.

2. Addressing Disparities: Identifying and addressing systemic barriers, socioeconomic disparities, and structural inequalities that limit access to memory enhancement resources and perpetuate health disparities.

Balancing Memory Enhancement with Personal Autonomy and Identity

Memory enhancement interventions raise complex ethical questions about the impact on personal autonomy, identity, and authenticity. While memory enhancement may improve cognitive function and enhance learning capabilities, it also raises concerns about the potential alteration of personal memories, experiences, and identity. Some ethical considerations include:

1. Preservation of Authenticity: Respecting individuals' autonomy and preserving their authentic identity, experiences, and memories while considering the potential impact of memory enhancement interventions on personal identity and self-concept.

2. Personal Choice and Agency: Recognizing individuals' right to make autonomous decisions about memory enhancement interventions based on their values, preferences, and goals, while respecting diverse perspectives and cultural norms regarding memory and identity.

3. Ethical Oversight and Regulation: Implementing ethical oversight mechanisms, professional guidelines, and regulatory frameworks to ensure responsible development, deployment, and use of memory enhancement technologies in accordance with ethical principles and societal values.

In summary, addressing the ethical considerations in memory enhancement requires a multifaceted approach that prioritizes safety, autonomy, privacy, equity, and respect for human dignity. By engaging stakeholders, fostering dialogue, and integrating ethical principles into research, policy, and practice, we can navigate the complex ethical landscape of memory enhancement and promote ethical innovation that benefits individuals and society as a whole.

Chapter 10: Practical Applications of Memory Techniques

Memory techniques offer powerful tools for enhancing cognitive abilities, improving learning outcomes, and optimizing performance in various fields. From education and training to professional endeavours and personal development, the practical applications of memory techniques are diverse and far-reaching. This chapter explores how memory techniques can be applied effectively in different contexts, including education, professional settings, and personal growth.

Applying Memory Techniques in Various Fields

Memory techniques, also known as mnemonic strategies, leverage cognitive processes to enhance memory encoding, retention, and retrieval. These techniques involve the use of mnemonic devices, visualization, association, and repetition to make information more memorable and easier to recall. Practical applications of memory techniques include:

1. Education: Memory techniques are invaluable tools for students of all ages and academic levels. By employing mnemonic devices, such as acronyms, visualization techniques, and memory palaces, students can improve their retention of key concepts, vocabulary, and factual information across diverse subjects.

2. Professional Development: Professionals in various fields, including healthcare, education, business, and public speaking, can benefit from memory techniques to enhance productivity, communication, and decision-making skills. Memory techniques can help professionals remember important details, protocols, procedures, and client information more effectively.

3. Personal Development: Memory techniques can also be applied to personal development goals, such as learning new languages, acquiring new skills, or memorizing inspirational quotes and passages. By incorporating memory techniques into daily routines and learning activities, individuals can expand their knowledge, boost creativity, and sharpen cognitive abilities.

Memory Enhancement in Education and Training

In the field of education and training, memory techniques play a critical role in facilitating learning, retention, and academic success. Teachers, educators, and trainers can incorporate memory-enhancing strategies into instructional design, curriculum development, and classroom activities to support student learning and achievement. Practical applications of memory enhancement in education and training include:

1. Active Learning: Encouraging active learning strategies, such as concept mapping, mnemonics, and retrieval practice, promotes student engagement, comprehension, and long-term memory retention.

2. Visual Aids: Using visual aids, diagrams, charts, and multimedia resources can enhance memory encoding and facilitate understanding of complex concepts and relationships.

3. Scaffolding: Providing scaffolding and support structures, such as outlines, summaries, and study guides, helps students organize information and reinforce memory consolidation.

Memory Techniques for Professionals

Professionals in various fields can leverage memory techniques to enhance job performance, communication skills, and decision-making abilities. Practical applications of memory techniques for professionals include:

1. Healthcare Workers: Healthcare professionals, including doctors, nurses, and medical students, can use memory techniques to remember patient details, medical terminology, treatment protocols, and diagnostic criteria more effectively.

2. Educators: Teachers, professors, and educational professionals can incorporate memory techniques into lesson planning, instructional delivery, and assessment strategies to promote student engagement, comprehension, and academic success.

3. Public Speakers: Public speakers, presenters, and communicators can utilize memory techniques, such as visualization, storytelling, and rehearsal strategies, to deliver compelling presentations, speeches, and lectures that resonate with audiences and leave a lasting impression.

Using Memory Techniques for Personal Growth and Development

Memory techniques offer valuable tools for personal growth, self-improvement, and lifelong learning. Individuals can harness the power of memory techniques to expand their knowledge, develop new skills, and achieve personal goals. Practical applications of memory techniques for personal growth include:

1. *Learning New Skills:* Whether mastering a musical instrument, acquiring a new language, or honing a craft, memory techniques can expedite the learning process and enhance skill acquisition.

2. *Memorization:* Memorizing inspirational quotes, poems, passages, or historical dates using memory techniques can enrich personal experiences, foster creativity, and stimulate intellectual curiosity.

3. *Cognitive Fitness:* Engaging in memory exercises, brain teasers, and mental challenges can promote cognitive fitness, improve memory recall, and maintain mental acuity as individuals age.

Dr. Pooja Agarwal

In conclusion, memory techniques offer versatile and practical applications across various fields, including education, professional development, and personal growth. By incorporating memory-enhancing strategies into daily routines, learning activities, and professional endeavours, individuals can optimize their cognitive abilities, expand their knowledge base, and achieve greater success in their personal and professional lives.

Conclusion

Throughout this journey exploring memory development, enhancement techniques, and practical applications, we have delved into the fascinating realm of human cognition and the intricate workings of memory. As we conclude our exploration, let us recap key concepts and techniques, encourage continuous practice and improvement, emphasize the importance of memory in personal and professional success, and empower individuals to take control of their memory and cognitive health.

Recap of Key Concepts and Techniques

In our exploration, we have uncovered a myriad of memory enhancement techniques, including mnemonic strategies, visualization, association, repetition, and active learning. These techniques harness the power of our cognitive processes to encode, retain, and retrieve information more effectively. From memory palaces to spaced repetition, each technique offers unique advantages and applications across various domains of life.

Encouragement to Continue Practicing and Improving Memory Skills

Memory is a skill that can be honed and refined through practice and deliberate effort. Just as athletes train their bodies and musicians practice their instruments, individuals can train their minds and improve their memory skills. By incorporating memory exercises, brain games, and memory challenges into daily routines, individuals can stimulate neural pathways, enhance cognitive function, and sharpen memory recall abilities over time.

Importance of Memory in Personal and Professional Success

Memory plays a pivotal role in personal and professional success, influencing learning, problem-solving, decision-making, and communication abilities. Whether in academic pursuits, career advancement, or everyday interactions, a strong memory can enhance efficiency, productivity, and effectiveness. Individuals with well-developed memory skills are better equipped to absorb new information, adapt to changing circumstances, and thrive in dynamic environments.

Empowerment to Take Control of Memory and Cognitive Health

Empowering individuals to take control of their memory and cognitive health is essential for promoting lifelong learning, mental well-being, and quality of life. By adopting healthy lifestyle habits, engaging in cognitive activities, and seeking opportunities for intellectual growth and stimulation, individuals can support brain health, prevent cognitive decline, and optimize memory performance throughout the lifespan. Moreover, staying socially engaged, maintaining physical fitness, managing stress, and getting adequate sleep are critical factors that contribute to overall cognitive vitality.

In conclusion, memory is not merely a passive storage system but a dynamic cognitive process that shapes our experiences, knowledge, and identities. By embracing the power of memory and cultivating memory skills, individuals can unlock new potentials, expand their horizons, and enrich their lives in profound ways. Let us continue to explore, discover, and harness the boundless possibilities of memory, embracing its transformative power to enhance our personal and professional endeavours. As we embark on this journey, may we seize every opportunity to nurture our memory and cognitive health,

Dr. Pooja Agarwal

empowering ourselves and others to thrive in a world shaped by the extraordinary capabilities of the human mind.